EMBODIMENTS
Of
TRUTH

Geraldine Guy

Embodiments of Truth ~ Geraldine Guy

ISBN-13: 978-0692226568

ISBN: 10: 0692226567

Library of Congress Control Number: 2014941734

Genre: Inspirational, Spiritual and Devotional

Published By: Reading Between The Lines Publishing

Email: readingbetweenthelinespublishing@gmail.com

Website: http://www.readingbetweenthelinespublishing.com

Website: http://www.geraldineguy.webbly.com

Photo on the front of the book cover: RBTLPublishing

Book Cover: Reading Between The Line Publishing

Editors/Proofreaders: Reading Between The

Lines Publishing & Lee Taylor

Content Editor: Reading Between The Lines Publishing

DEDICATION

This book is dedicated to my husband, Robert Guy of 47 years. To my daughter, Robin Guy and also my granddaughter Victoria Herron, whom I love dearly.

Embodiments of Truth ~ Geraldine Guy

ACKNOWLEDGMENTS

Geraldine Guy expresses much love and sincere thanks to:

God for being the strength of my life and for the gift of creativity and for giving me a passion to write. Thank You Almighty God.

I would also like to thank my daughter, Robin Guy who has supported and encouraged my every endeavor in every way, who is also my secretary, assistant, and best friend.

To Wardell Thomas, for teaching me about the spiritual laws of light and darkness and to Pastor George L. Parks for being my spiritual leader.

To Cynthia Newsome for her unshakable faith in me and for causing me to believe in myself; also for being my motivator, and to everyone everywhere that is reading what I've shared from the bowels of my heart that you'll have an opened mind to let the "Truth be Truth."

INTRODUCTION

Geraldine Guy is one of the world's most word conscious women. Her expression of words reveals the truth about real life problems. Guy endeavors to make a powerful impact and difference in the world because she has recognized that people are oppressed, while burdened with worries and anxieties, simply because they have been deceived by the powers of darkness.

She's faced many problems, obstacles, and disappointments and has met many challenges. Her life has been threatened many times because of chronic illness. Now Guy would like to convey her message through her writing, how the spiritual laws of light and darkness has caused her to change her focus and bring forth the reality of who she really is! Although experience has been her best teacher, and meeting a man who was much wiser and full of knowledge about the only true and living God has brought Guy to a point of truth, absolute truth, where she no longer uses spiritual incorrect words that gives power to death and draws us closer to the cemetery.

She also declares that when we fully understand that the evening and the morning are a day, then we will understand the power of words and the power they give to death. Guy believes that we give honor to darkness in many ways that we are not fully conscious of, and the manifestation of it is crime, illness, and death.

Embodiments of Truth, is not just an ordinary book of poetry. However it includes detailed accounts and sayings with the intent of enhancing our lives while it will grow us spiritually and raise our consciousness levels to all new heights and depths. Embodiments of Truth is truth, it is powerful, poignant, and thought provoking that offers a fresh insight into a world of opportunities, a glimpse into the realities of life, poetry that communicates with its readers, as they gain a new perspective on love, hatred, spirituality that is in our society.

You will read, "The Burning Bush President" where Guy exposes people in power because she knows that people in power not only diminish our spirits, but lower our standards of living. You will also read, "The Lie that No Longer Exists", "Exposing the Truth of Who We Really Are", "When Love Hurts, and Leaving Me without An Invitation". You will hear many cries and praises to God, her response to family and friends on their joyous occasions or their Walk through the Valley. My ultimate goal is to help others to encourage, enrich and empower their lives.

Embodiments of Truth ~ Geraldine Guy

Embodiments of Truth ~ Geraldine Guy

CONTENTS

CONTENTS

CONTENTS

Embodiments of Truth ~ Geraldine Guy

CONTENTS

Embodiments of Truth ~ Geraldine Guy

CONTENTS

CONTENTS

CONTENTS

CONTENTS

CHAPTER 1
"Life"

The most important thing a person possesses is one's life. However, since we are spiritually incorrect in our words, we are giving more power to death than life. Therefore, we have made death the ruler of the world, meaning we have made death larger than life.

Death cannot be larger than life. Most of us are so comfortable in our belief about God that we have no concept of how using spiritual incorrect words gives power to death. We live by the spiritual laws of light and darkness.

All of our words are associated with either light or darkness. Light is one with life and darkness is one with death. Since life and death is in the powers of a man's tongue, the words for life are in your mouth. Proverbs Chapter 18 verse 21:

Words are our access to life. Therefore, words of light have to be brought forth in our conversation in order to bring forth a God of Light. You are justified or condemned by your words.

Matthew Chapter 12 verse 37, *"**Don't let your words condemn you**"*. The word itself separates darkness from light. When you become conscious of words, your words will proceed from the mouth of the living God and your words begin to say what God says about you and not what your five senses tell you. All darkness can do is follow light. I am light and darkness cannot comprehend light. We are children of light and the day; we are no longer children of the night. (Thessalonians Chapter 5:5)

Notice that the word, "I am" says that I am light. I am healed, blessed, and full of knowledge, wisdom and love. These words cause you to be one with God. The word, "I was" is in the past.

CHAPTER 2
My Journey To A Victorious Recovery

The next few pages invites you into my heart and gives you a reflection of my most inner most feelings, although there were times when I would write out of other people's pain. However, there would be times when I would feel deeply agitated in my mind or trouble in my heart and it would always come out in my writing that I couldn't acknowledge my needs being met.

I knew enough to keep holding on to the promise. I knew that God had promised me life and life has everything you need. I had reached a point of truth and had refused to let myself get depressed for I knew depression was spiritually incorrect and it means to see now way out! I have admitted already that I would sometimes be distressed and I knew it was only a moment, I knew joy would come in the morning.

The winter of 2010, I was hospitalized for severe chest pain with my heart racing out of control. I remember shimmering and gasping for breath while trying to focus on life. However, I was too weak to hold my focus, as I was having too many complications. It was about three a.m., when a nurse came into my room to take my vital signs. I somehow found the strength to ask for a pen and paper as if I had seen a vision of things to come. I had written it as if it had already happened and as a result, I was feeling like a new person the very next day. It brought me back to this truth: *"to know God expands your mind above believing in death."*

CHAPTER 3
"REMOVING THE MOUNTAIN"

I want to thank God that my crisis has passed. Thank You God Almighty that the illness didn't linger, nor did it last. I must take some credit that the illness didn't stay, but it was the devastator of each agonizing day. I had some problems with my breast, the heart too I must confess and the throbbing in my head was like the sounds of a drum, it was all I could do to keep my feeble body from going numb.

Death had once more knocked at my door, it was to leave empty handed just like before. I had to do what I had to do to depend on the truth to see me through. I would ascend up to the hills of the Lord; until I am planted like a tree by the sea and know that death cannot consume me, but I want to make one thing crystal clear; faith only comes if you can hear.

I attended to thy words that were life and health to my flesh. I drank the waters that quenches all thirst and filled my spirit enough to burst. While walking through my fiery trials, my spirit began transforming visions before my eyes, knowing a vision is where my future lies.

Now that glorious day has come to be, sickness and infirmity can no longer triumph over me, for my greatest honor was finding victory over thee and casting that mountain into the sea. Once again, I want to thank thee!

CHAPTER 4
"Do You Know Me? Who Am I?

Do you really know me? Do you really know my powers? Do you know that if you have faith, I can change any situation within the hour?

Do you know the miracles that I have done and that there is not a fight that I haven't won? I can do all things and whatsoever joy you need I can bring.

I can give you the power to create wealth and cause you to walk in divine health. I can take the sting of death and create in you everlasting breath! I can cause your visions to come true, and in the times of storm, I can see you through.

I can make you the head and not the tail. I can take away your sorrows and make you the giver and not the borrower. I am that I am! I am God Almighty. I parted the red sea and set my people free. I am the Lord, Thy God.

I created The Throne of Grace. I Am the one that can take you to a never dreamed of place. I created the Heaven and the earth. I planted the seed that gave you birth. Your sins I freely forgave and your soul I did save.

Hearken unto me, give me your hand, and I will lead you to the Promised Land.

CHAPTER 5
"Reality of Faith"

Everyone wants to believe that they walk by faith, but the truth is that everyone walks by sight. Faith is the substance of things hoped for, the assurance of reality. Faith is understanding. You cannot believe anything that you do not understand.

It's proof of things unseen. It causes things that are not as though they were already in sight. Hence, I believe in life although I am only seeing death manifest around me because I understand God's plan for man is "life".

Faith is advancing from death to life; it will take you beyond the realm of your five senses and force you to make a shift in consciousness.

To a point of spiritually understanding instead of physically understanding, as you give birth to the spirit. Romans, Chapter 1 verse 17: *"for therein is the righteousness of God revealed from faith to faith, as it is written the just shall live by faith"*. Faith introduces us to the unseen world.

CHAPTER 6
"If You Have Faith"

If you have faith when trouble comes like a flood. You'll keep remembering that you are under the blood. If you have faith when it seems that you can no longer stand, your faith will keep you holding the Father's hand.

If you have faith, you'll never fear or doubt, for you would know that God is with you, you will never be without.

If you have faith, you'll know God is there, and you'll place yourself in his loving care. For your faith let's you see the love he has to give, and all you have to do is realize that and live!

So, if you have faith and have suffered grief and pain, keep on praying in the Father's name!

CHAPTER 7
"When Light Is At Hand"

When we are conscious of the spiritual laws of light and darkness, we have a reminder, a state of conscious that lets us know when darkness is lurking.

Remember life is of the day. The truth of God is in our words, as we live or die by our words. The laws of God are word laws. Just as we are punished for breaking man's laws, the result of breaking word laws, is: "death".

When we stay into the day of the Lord with our words, our minds are controlled by light causing us to walk after the spirit. Darkness has one job and that is to kill. Whereas, light's job is to keep us alive.

Consider this example; the media gave special attention to a four month old child and her struggle for life after she had been accidentally left in a daycare van, where the temperature reached as high as one hundred and twenty degrees.

Ironically, the child lived for two days. While the law officials tried to decide if the driver of the daycare van was to blame. However, everyone that uses the word, "night and kids" in their conversation gives power to death. These words are spiritually incorrect and they give power to death. Therefore, the driver had to have the words, "night and kids" in her conversation and the child had to be left as a kid in the van.

Otherwise, the child would have been left in the light of the driver's mind and she would have remembered the child because of knowing a God of light.

Our children are being taken away from us every day because in our words, we are calling them "kids" and our words are causing them to manifest as animals.

Animals are raised and killed. Consider this truth from *Proverbs Chapter 22 verse 6 "Train up a child in the way that he should go, and when he is old, he will not depart from it"*.

Children should not be called "kids", nor should they be raised. Thus, they should be trained. Under Moses Law, "kids" were goats and was used as a sin offering. Your words should not have you trapped under Moses law.

CHAPTER 8
"Examining the Bible"

Let's examine the Bible and scriptures. The Bible is a book about God, but it is not God. The Bible was not written to be understood with our physical minds, it was written as a script to be acted out with our spiritual minds. Otherwise, it will remain a mystery to most of us until a true preacher comes along and act out the script.

The scriptures of the Bible represent a script, as part in a play or movie. The producers of any play or movie know that they cannot begin to produce a play or movie without a written script or a guideline to go by. They know exactly what they are looking for. Hundreds of people may be called in for a tryout, but the part may only call for one or two people. When the casting call is over, the producers select the best person for the part. In the same manner, the Bible tells us that many are called but few are chosen.

Was the preacher called or chosen for his part? Is he acting it out according to the script? There are many who will not get the part because they do not understand the script. The reality of not understanding the script is darkness *(ignorance).* Therefore, the written script of the Bible has not been acted out despite the many different characters that have come forward to try out for the part. An article was once printed in one of our local papers about one of our most prominent leaders who was being praised for being one of the greatest preachers in the world.

What constitutes a great preacher? Has life come forward as the result of a great preacher? Has crime decreased? Has the over population of our prison came under control? Has poverty declined? Is the sick picking up their beds and walking as the result of one of the greatest preachers in the world or have we confused great entertainment with preaching of the gospel?

This is not to condemn the preacher for our problems. However, we do need to understand how we honor darkness and give power to death. I have had many people tell me they have a great preacher because he preaches from the Bible.

They have no knowledge of the carnality of the preacher's mind and cannot differentiate if he is preaching from his physical mind or if his words are proceeding from the mouth of God, which is the spirit.

They are moved by what sounds good and the scriptures are pleasing to their ears. Words that are proceeding from the mouth of man cannot lead you any further than the grave and they keep you trapped in the same old concepts and traditions that you have always known. We cannot live out of old concepts and traditions because they have passed, you cannot hold on to the past and live! Remember, God is *"meaning now"*, *today!* You will never find God in the past. God is a God of life. Life is one with light and knowledge. Knowledge and light does not stand still. A real preacher brings forth the power of God on earth.

A physical preacher focuses on life after death, as he is death conscious, therefore, he can only bring forth or manifest death, which is the main reason we see so much death manifesting everyday on earth. God's will is that you live and you must know what life "is", because if you don't know what life "is, then you don't know who God is.

CHAPTER 9
"Identifying a True Preacher"

From this point on we are going to let truth be truth, which is to say, let God be truth. Romans, Chapter 3 verse 4: *"Let God be true, but every man a liar".* The church have been a deception to many people who believe they have been hearing from the word of God, when they have been hearing from the mouth of man, which is of no effect nor does it create God's kind of faith and love.

Romans Chapter 10 verses 14-15: *"How can the people hear without a preacher and the preacher cannot preach except he is sent"* Who did God send to preach his word? How do we identify a real preacher?

While it is true, faith comes by hearing. However, faith in God only comes by hearing the word of God. Words that are proceeding from the mouth of man will only create a cycle of death. That is why everyone believes in death instead of life.

I have met too many people who are too comfortable in their physical understanding about the church and the preacher. They have mistakenly taken what sounds good and scripture pleasing to their ears to be of God.

People look for God in many different doctrines and beliefs, but God can only be found through the truth of his word. People are moved by what they see with their eyes. The big picture deceives people. Hence, one of the most largest and beautiful church a where the crowd and money are. The well-dressed preacher who has the authority to divide their followers.

Thus, in order to conquer you must first divide. This way the preacher can conquer the people minds to rule over them. Like the Government, the preacher legalized force such as guilt to destroy value because they know that emotions are a real part of every person.

Some ministries use the pulpit to pull people into the pit with their words, the pit being the grave. Consider this example: a detective is trained to solve a crime or detect something that is hidden, In like manner; we need to be trained to solve the mystery of the church and the preacher.

The following is just a few questions that you will need to start your investigation with. These questions will raise your consciousness about the truth of the church and the preacher.

1. *Is the preacher one with what he is saying? This is important because the only way you can hear by the word of God is for the preacher to preach God's word and know that God is a God of life. Light and life agree as one. Remember faith comes by hearing. We have faith in many things that we hear, but faith in God comes by hearing the word of God.*

2. Does the preacher understand that he and God are one and the same? Another important factor because it allows the preacher to preach from his spirit instead of the carnality of his mind. The truth of God is only preached from the spirit.

3. Is the preacher preaching life? First and foremost important because the hearers of the word can only believe and manifest what they are hearing. This is the evidence that will convict any preacher because it is totally impossible for a preacher to preach life if he believes in death, this is the absolute truth. It does not matter how good he sounds.

God is life, you are either one with life *(light)* or you are one with darkness *(death)*. The preaching of death have been manifesting in the earth as the result of what people are believing in and what they have been hearing. It is spiritual that light has power over darkness. Darkness cannot comprehend light, nor can you bury light.

The truth of God's word has the power to change the problems that is plaguing America and the world; because the truth forces us into spiritual laws, which is to say forces us into reality and helps us understand that America has come under word judgment; because of our rejection of knowledge and because we have been spiritually incorrect in our words. Understanding life is spiritual, however, the highest degree of education without understanding is physical; it is lifeless.

Proverbs Chapter 3 verse 13: We find these words, *"Happy is the man that finds wisdom and the man that gets understanding".*

- There are many benefits in life that goes with wisdom and understanding. Wisdom is not a result of any education or physical effort; it is a gift from God.

James Chapter 1 verse 5: *"If any of you lack wisdom, let him ask of God".* The reality of sin is not what you do, but what you say out of your mouth.

CHAPTER 10
"You Shall Know the Truth"

If you will listen, I'll explain a simple truth told so plain. You must have a listening ear, one with wisdom to hear. You must be able to believe what you are about to receive.

Contrary to what you think you know. There are many religious concepts that you must let go. Truth is simple, but somewhat deep, and can't be figured out while you sleep.

Truth makes you free, who can deny. If you could listen and then reply. Truth will raise your consciousness to a new level of height. As you take your walk by faith and not by sight. Now, this is how the story goes.

Some will doubt, but who really knows. It's all about the problems that are plaguing the earth, and having to do with truth bringing forth birth. I am talking about the problems that man can no longer subdue.

Problems our political leaders know not what to do. Who has the answer that was lost somewhere in the birth of time, when a lie was told to all mankind!

CHAPTER 11
"Appearing to be a People of Color"

Hosea, Chapter 4 verse 6: God tell us, *"my people are destroyed from a lack of knowledge, because thou have rejected knowledge, I'll also reject thee"*. Light, knowledge, and life agree as one. Knowledge overcomes ignorance as light overcomes darkness, and the truth overcomes a lie. John, Chapter 8 verse 32: *"You shall know the truth and the truth shall make you free"*.

If you have not been hearing by the word based on the evidence that light has uncovered for you, you have been deceived about who you really are. Truth always adds up and it makes sense. However, you cannot make a lie fit. Hence, black and white doesn't fit.

The word "and" separates and puts racial divisions among the people of the world, which have been deceived about the issues of black and white. They are deceived because it is impossible to teach what one doesn't know.

Nor is it possible for our leaders to lead where they don't go. Truth begins with your admitting you don't know the answer and being willing to challenge your old beliefs and concepts. We cannot continue this journey into darkness. It will only lead us to destruction. The reality of what I am saying comes from the spirituality of knowing who "I am". Black people don't know who they are so they have bought a bill of goods that is not working because it is based upon a lie.

Darkness will cause you to walk as a blind man. Hence, if you trusted someone to bring you a dog and they brought you a goat instead. You took the goat out every day and the goat never barked or chased a rabbit, how long would it take you to figure out it's not a dog, it's a goat!

In like manner, someone looked at the color of dark appearance people's skin color and told them they were black. I have heard people say, "I am black and I am proud".

However, if you see yourself as a black person; you are in agreement with a lie. There is no such thing as black people. Truth is based on the spiritual laws of light and darkness. Black is darkness, ignorance, and death. Light is based on knowing, knowledge, and life.

Therefore, if you see yourself as a black person, you have separated from the kingdom of light, knowledge, and life. White people cast the same dark shadow as black people. A shadow is one with death. A shadow is one with a lie, sin, the devil, and death. They too don't know how to overcome their shadows, which is death. Webster defines black, without light, that which is dark, dirty, evil, wicked, and sad. Black relates to everything of darkness. Hence, blackmail is to lose money to prevent information that would bring shame or disgrace.

Blackout means to lose consciousness. Black is the color of mourning. As you can see only connection with black causes some sort of lost. Black, darkness, and night are one and the same, which is one with death. God is light.

There is no darkness in him. When emphasis is placed on anything other than light, we give power to such things as violent crimes, AIDS, cancer, and flood, things that leads us to death. Black is the absence of light.

However, God is a God of light. There is no darkness in him. Why would anyone want to identify with black and how long will it take you to figure out who you really are?

CHAPTER 12
"The Lie that no Longer Exist"

This is a truth only a few people know, it is a lie told about being a Negro. Some may come and some may go, but how many shared a truth that the people needed to know all about a lie started so very long ago. How could you have room for your spirit to grow or have a reason for becoming a hero, when you were told that you were just a Negro?

Just because you were told that you were black, you bought a bill of goods that you have refused to take back, for you can't be black and free, it is a joke don't you see! We cannot be black and come together as a whole. It is a lie that your slave masters have forever told.

Yes, many believing to be African American have come forward so rich, bold, and brave, but the lie still led them no further than the grave. So here is a truth that you should comprehend and save, the ignorance of being Black is what caused you to be a slave.

Now who can deny that we have lived a lie? Thinking that we were black and had to die? Black is only a disguise, it's only what you see when you look with your eyes.

Webster will tell you that black is a word, a word that is defeated, as long as you are trying to be black, you will never beat it! You cannot remain black. Otherwise, who will you be when darkness leaves and never comes back.

If you are black, you are alone, for God never took darkness and claimed it as his own. We must overcome the issue of race despite the obstacles we have to face.

For we know that if we come together as never before, we would still open another closed door! And we can no longer be denied our true identity or equality, as Martin Luther King dream becomes a reality.

Yes, freedom has rung and will continue to ring,
As we surpass the freedom that the spirit of truth shall bring. As the struggle continues and we accomplish one more spiritual event, always thanking God for the truth that he sent.

We have come this far by grace, how can we not overcome the issues of race? We have put forth such effort to bring this change, how degrading it would have been, how much shame, for we as African American to remain the same.

CHAPTER 13
"Fantasy of Holidays"

(Psalms Chapter 118 verse 24)

This is the day, which the Lord hath made; we will rejoice and be glad in it. As God said, "If it was not made in the beginning, it was not made". A holiday was not made in the beginning. They were later created out of the laws of man. Although billions of dollars are spent each year in honor of a day that's nothing less than a fantasy, it's an empty, lifeless day that gives darkness the power it needs to bring forth more crime and death.

Holidays were originally created as a day to celebrate some sort of event of the past. The past is darkness and is one with death. Holidays are spiritually incorrect and they fight against "life", as the word, holiday derives from the word hollow meaning empty, void, and worthless.

These words keep you out of the day of the Lord. There is nothing spiritual about a holiday. Nothing at all, no matter how we justify the celebration, we are honoring darkness.

Martin Luther King birthday celebration came about because of his death. Elvis Presley became more famous after death. We have established that a holiday is one with darkness and death. Now, let's consider this example: The reality of celebrating a birthday is celebrating the process of deterioration caused by aging, the reason we grow old and die. However, we age because our minds stop growing, as you cannot grow believing in death.

This is not to say you should not have your celebration, as life is a giver and "life" will not take anything from you. The world system takes advantage of these shopper's days and feed off the people's ignorance. More stores are opening earlier and staying open later and more people are asked to work on a holiday.

For many, these days bring forth depression, as many cannot afford to buy and celebrate and those who can afford to celebrate holidays are committing acts of darkness, which is one with death. Therefore, holidays need to be spiritually corrected to the word, "holyday", as God have said, "Remember the Sabbath day to keep it holy". Holy day do not honor the dead, they honor "life"!

CHAPTER 14
"The Love for Money Mentality"

Acts Chapter 8 verse 20 *"But Peter said unto him, thy money perishes with thee, because thou hast thought that the gift of God may be purchased with money."* The love for money is the root cause of most of the problems that are plaguing America. We live in a society that is run solely on money, as the world is being controlled by the money exchangers.

While it is true that money can buy most anything we want, it's still a deception. It creates a false image of what life is and robs you of your self-identity taking away your individuality. You cannot be one with "life" or you cannot enter into "life" when you are one with money.

Money hides the reality of who you really are, as we can appear to change from being a nobody to being a somebody depending on the amount of money we may come into, as some become professional athletes, actors, rap artists, and etc.

Hence, money took O.J. Simpson to the top and caused him to appear to be somebody that he was not. Michael Vick was charged with conspiracy in interstate commerce and aiding or unlawful animal fighting venture and was sentenced to twenty-three months federal time. He is just one of the athletes

Embodiments of Truth ~ Geraldine Guy

who were making millions of dollars. This is to say that money could be the answer to the many things that we desire or lust after.

However, it cannot buy the things we need. Needs are spiritual and are supplied by God. Hence, money will buy a house, but all the money in the world cannot buy a home. It will buy any kind of bed you want, but not the rest you need. It will buy all kinds of food and yet it cannot buy you an appetite. It will buy lots of fun, but not happiness.

CHAPTER 15
"Precept of Male & Female"

(Genesis Chapter 1 verse 27)

So God created man in his own image, in the image of God created he him, male and female created he them. Have you not read that he, which made them at the beginning, made them male and female?

Jesus thought in parables, a parable being something used physical to explain something in the spirit, as parables are given to know the mystery of the kingdom of God, Isaiah Chapter 28 verse 10 says: ***"For precept must be upon precept, precept upon precept, line upon line, have a little and there a little"***. Precepts are from God, it's knowing the law and knowing its' intent.

Precept: A man and woman "is" of the earth whereas, a male and female is of the spirit. Jesus wrote on the ground because the woman was of the earth. A male walks after the spirit, (walking after who you really are) who God created you to be! We have already established that in the beginning God created male and female. God tells us that if it was not made in the beginning, it was not made. This is to say that darkness created man and woman.

Embodiments of Truth ~ Geraldine Guy

A man and woman have sex, having sex creates acts of darkness, diseases, unwanted pregnancies, rape, babies born with abnormalities, and etc. Therefore having sex is not in the bible because the concept of having sex is too small for "life". For Life is the biggest concept you can get into your head. Only a man and a woman can and will have sex and create acts of darkness.

Hence, a man can rape a woman, but a male cannot rape a female. A male and a female know each other, as Joseph knew Mary, which is to say a spiritual minded man tries to enter your thoughts first!

CHAPTER 16
"The Need for Spiritual Growth"

Most of us are over extending our lives mostly because we have put wants before needs. Needs are spiritual; and are supplied by God. Whereas, wants are physical and are added after seeking the Kingdom of God first.

If we are addicted to materialistic things, it is usually because we feel the need to have more. So we can feel better off. When we don't know who we are in God, we find ourselves always trying to feel a void adding unnecessary stress and anxieties to our lives.

We have all heard of the millennium or the end of the world or a new beginning. It is a change, it is reversing priorities. The things we consider least must be first. For example, if our focus is on money and things; it can buy such as designer bags, shoes, cars, houses, and etc. Then it must converse to God and life, which is one and the same.

We are living in perilous times and are always struggling with the wiles of the devil and unless we advance spiritual, we will not understand that we are experiencing symptoms of a spiritual problem.

However, in order to grow spiritual, we must first

understand the spiritual laws of light and darkness. Light is of the day and is one with God. Light and life are one and the same. Darkness is of the night and is one with death. Everything we do is either associated with light or darkness.

Therefore, our focus and investment must be totally in life. There is a need to listen and obey our spirits, as our problems should determine our agenda. We all have conversations about wanting to have something in life. However, seeking to have something in life causes you to leave life behind. Life has everything you need.

CHAPTER 17
"MY WALK THROUGH THE VALLEY"

Through the valley I once walked, problems and circumstances were all my talk. God's word in my heart I did not hide, and I stumbled getting to the other side.

I did not know that divine healing for my spirit, mind, and body was available to me, because I wouldn't take my eyes off my circumstances and look up to Thee.

And all because I did not seek him, my way through the valley grew so dim. Just when I thought the valley was too dark to cope, the spirit of the Lord fell upon me and gave me hope.

When I heard about the Holy Ghost and how it would teach, the end of the valley I began to reach. I delighted myself in the word of God, and began to speak God's promises in my heart, and when at times I fell by the wayside, I drew up the word I had hid inside. It was only when I took my eyes off of my sorrow and pain, I can began to use the authority I had in His name! For in the valley you do not stay, you only walk through is what I pray.

CHAPTER 18
"A New Beginning"

A new beginning I could not find, for negative thoughts had conquered my mind. I looked for God high and I looked for him low, but I still had thoughts that I couldn't let go. I really thought God was moving too slow, because all my dreams would come and go.

It was like being in a dessert of hot sand, looking for an oasis and only finding dry land. So often I would cry and then I would smile, for I knew I had to go that extra mile.

My heart began to open, to the truth that had been spoken, and my wounded heart, that was once torn apart.

Started to recall all the things that were available to us all, and then I saw His face, and I knew that a beginning had taken place.

CHAPTER 19
"WHO AM I?"

I am one with God and He is one with me. I'll forever surrender to victory, my oneness has set me free, and all I am, I owe to Thee!

I am part of my Father's perfect plan. I am not ruled by the laws of the land. I am a new person in the earth; I am the salt that purifies the new birth. I am the light that men can see; the Kingdom of Heaven is brought forth in me. I am Abraham's seed; I am everything that this world needs.

I am like a tree planted by the sea, rivers of waters flowing within me. I am the Son of God. I am so far ahead; I am separating myself from among the dead. I am controlling my destiny and I am taking my place in eternity.

I am born of the spirit and not of the flesh, walking in truth knowing I am blessed.

I am Geraldine and I am real, therefore, my name is Geraldine Isreal.

CHAPTER 20
"The Manifestation of my Wish"

I use to wish I could sing. I couldn't and thought that was a terrible thing. I use to wish I could pray, but never knew exactly what words to say.

I use to wish I could write a poem, but no words could I shape or form I use to wish I had fame, but people barely knew my name.

I use to wish I had money, I didn't and people thought that was funny! I use to wish I had a friend for I didn't want to be alone and I didn't believe I was wrong. Now without hesitation, and a long road of dedication.

I have something worth more than silver or gold; I have peace in my soul.

CHAPTER 21
"THE ANSWER"

I might not be an angel at least not in your sight and I don't always do exactly what is right, but I still operate from the power of the light. Some think they know me, but they are only moved on what they see, little do they know I am not what I seem to be, I am more like a tree planted by the sea.

You won't read about me in any kind of a book and the truth about me surely you have overlooked. So here is my story and it is true of how the light have seen me through. I am not black and I am not white. I am just a star shining as light, and if you can't see the shine, it is because night has conquered your mind. I cannot turn holy water to wine, still my conscious is too high to pay a fine, nor can I take the odor out of a skunk, but I can drink and never get drunk.

My material belonging is as small as a mustard seed; yet, I have more than I need. I cannot be figured out in your mind, and you can't labor me with any kind of a crime. I can go anywhere and anytime I want to, I already know the things I need to know, and if you have things that you can't do, it is because you don't have the light to see you through.

CHAPTER 22
"THE PRESSURES OF LIFE"

God, who is one of a kind, come quick and ease my troubled mind. My life has been turned upside down, and it seems as though you are nowhere to be found. I have been through storm after storm. Now, I beg you to silence them so I can move on.

Maybe, I am responsible for these stumbling blocks, but was it enough to cause my blessings to stop!

I want to walk where the waters are still, but most of all: I want my empty cup filled. If you, but lead me to greener pastures, and somehow undo this total disaster. For I keep stretching my hands to thee, knowing that your plan was for me to be free. Lord, I have sought you diligently with my whole heart. Surely, these pressures of life cannot be my reward.

Because of your goodness and mercy, I have been washed ashore, but how long oh Lord? Before you hear my knock and open the door. How long will it be? Before you prepare my table of victory? The one I want prepared in the presence of my enemies.

And like a day of Pentecost, we all become friends. Lord, grant me this joyous feast, so from the pressures of life, I will be released.

CHAPTER 23
"Under the Anointing"

It was under the anointing that the spirit came, it changed my life and I was not the same. For once I was free from pain.

Under the anointing came the power of God, and it stirred up the gifts hid within my heart. Under the anointing, I could plainly see that the Lord had perfected all that concerned me.

The anointing mystified my mind, it was more than I could hope for, and more than I thought I could ever find.

No longer was I operating in the flesh, and I didn't think that I could ever settle for anything less.

Under the anointing I saw the miracles wrought by God's hand and began to understand his love for man.

I only saw God and what he was about. There was no room for the works of doubt.

I walked out of darkness into divine light; my days were no longer dark as night.

I am under the anointing to stay; I'll not walk back into yesterday.

CHAPTER 24
"Waiting on the Lord"

Lord, my head seems to always be bowed, and just to make sure you hear me, I cry out to you real loud.

Lord, I am part of the righteousness that shall inherit the land, but still feel the chastisement of your mighty hand.

What is the price I'll have to pay, for planting these bad seeds back in the day?

How long Oh, Lord, for these fiery trials? Please tell me they will be over in a short while.

Redeem me oh, Lord from the deep waters that are trying to overflow me, and plant me like a tree by the sea, as I put my trust in thee, for it was you Lord who created me.

CHAPTER 25
"A Promise Kept"

Oh God please don't chastise me in my sorrow, but let my blessing rise today and tomorrow.

My restless soul has been made whole for you Lord. I am humble now, I am part of the meek, who would guess, I was so weak.

I had asked for forgiveness for all the sin that I had wrought. I'm blessed now or so I thought, with the will to live, and living to give.

I now bow in prayer so all my burdens won't be too hard to bear.

CHAPTER 26
"Doubt and Fear"

Doubt and fear comes about, to keep you from finding God's way out. For doubt has a way of knowing how to keep your spirit from growing.

Doubt will make your life feel incomplete, for you can't have victory feeling defeat. Doubt cannot manifest your dreams. It can only make life worse than it seems.

Doubt will rob you of your smile, and take your strength to fight each trial. Doubt will cause discouragement, suffering, and pain; and you will forget God is near. For doubt will conquer faith and hope when the heart is filled with fear.

Stand on God's promise and don't be moved even when things seem hard to bear. Resist doubt, and say a faithful prayer. When doubt is in your heart and your fear is raised, lift up your head and sing a hymn of praise.

It's when doubt brings fear and make things go wrong, you need to use God's word to help you along. So, when the storms of life have tossed you about, use faith and erase the doubt.

CHAPTER 27
"If I Had a Dream"

I had a dream as impossible as it may seem. A dream that I thought was worth its weight in gold. One that couldn't be bought and couldn't be sold.

A dream that I thought would forever be told. But did I dream this dream at night? Without one bit of light. And how can this dream manifest when so deep did I sleep?

A dream that made me restless with my heart skipping beats. Sometimes there were bits and pieces that I could not recall. I had just dreamed and that was all. I dreamed as much as I thought I could. And not once did the dream help me or do me any good.

A dream that has awakened me, myself, and I. Crying and screaming why? I couldn't remember for no longer was I dreaming. For how can you dream when you're dreaming at "night"? I have never known darkness to bring forth light.

CHAPTER 28
"Foundation for Truth Is:"

A Church without Spot or Wrinkle

Foundation for Truth is not a tabernacle brought forth by the hands of a man. It was built upon a rock, a solid foundation that will forever stand. Foundation for Truth is a church brought forth by light. A church where there is no darkness and in your conversation there is no "night". Only in God, do you delight.

Foundation for Truth is the answer that people have searched for thick and thin. For it have brought forth the answer that lies within. Foundation for Truth brings forth the reality of "who", you really are, one with the sun, you are higher than a star.

It is not a church where tithes are paid, nor is it one where rules are made. It is a church brought forth by the words of a wise man. A church that's lead by God's guiding hand. A church that even, the simple can understand. A church where old concepts and traditions are left behind. A church that deals with the mentality of a man's mind. Is it the church that is coming forth without spot or wrinkle? It is not about being Baptist or water sprinkle. For how can you separate the water from the word?

Embodiments of Truth ~ Geraldine Guy

They are one, I am sure you have heard. It is not a church that you can join, silver and gold have it none, but it is a church where God's promise is life. There is no death and if you can't perceive this, somewhere on the rooftop you will be left.

So if you have agreed to fill your spiritual needs, Foundation for Truth is where you should plant your seeds!

CHAPTER 29
"Where Are Your Seeds?

Did you know that in the beginning God gave a seed? A seed that would supply your every need! A seed that produces after its' own kind. A seed that is planted in the spirituality of your own mind. And the only way that you can create a need is misplacing your seed. Do you have a need, where is your seed? So many times we cry out to God on our knees Lord help me, help me, please! But the Lord is going to say, How can I help you, you have no need and everything else is in your seed, where is your seed?

What have the seeds you've planted produced? Did they produce and bring forth the fruits of the spirit, or were they choked out by the thorns and weeds that ran wild and loose? Have you planted your seeds in darkness and are you reaping a harvest of carnality, or are you bringing forth true spirituality? Are your seeds bringing forth life or are they the ones producing enmity and strife? Is your seed a greed for silver and gold, one that you would have priced if it could be sold?

Where is your seed and what are your seeds producing? Are you bringing forth a seed of love or one of faith? Can you set a table of victory before you and celebrate? Where is your seed and whom did you give? If it's not in the kingdom how can you live?

CHAPTER 30
"What Is a Miracle?"

A miracle is God's way to achieve, what some people can't believe. A miracle mystifies the mind, and lets you know that there is a God of some kind.

A miracle comes when there is no way out, and it brings God's people out of doubt. A miracle is sometimes instantly and sometimes long, but it comes to make you strong. A miracle shows the power of God, and it helps people believe in their hearts.

A miracle fills a cup that runs dry, and makes you thank God, who is so high, but a miracle one should not plea, because it shows a sign of disbelief.

CHAPTER 31
"WHEN THE MOUTH SPEAKS"

When the mouth speaks, it should sanctify, glorify, and edify. For what proceeds out of the mouth is abundance in the heart, and it should always magnify the name of God.

When the mouth speaks, it should always speak words of faith, not words of doubt, for faith; has a way of bringing dreams about.

When the mouth speaks, tears should be dried and love should abide. Your words should always make someone that was giving up; want to drink from your cup. When the mouth speaks, it should not defile man; it should call those things that are not to make a stand.

When the mouth speaks, it should never speak words of malice or strife, it should only speak words of life. For it's the words you speak wherever you go, lifting other spirits and helping them grow.

CHAPTER 32
"The Place I Seek"

I am looking for a place I can't seem to find. It's a place that gives you the real meaning of a piece of mind. And shows you how to feel and live good in these critical times. A place I just can't seem to find.

This place is so incredible and it may be so far away. However, I need to have found it like yesterday. It's not heaven with the golden gates and it's not a place where you have to wait.

There are no streets paved in gold, it's just a place that helps your soul. And I feel sure or rather I know that this is a place I need to go where all my stress will be released, and my running mind will be at peace.

CHAPTER 33
"Desires of the Heart"

What is it that I most desire? I know it's something within me burning like a Holy Fire. Sometimes I laugh and sometimes I cry still wondering what is my real desire? What would really put my troubles at ease?

I have growing in me such a far-fetched search. Now, I am wondering if I have asked or wanted too much? Maybe I need something to give me wisdom and make me wise, or maybe it's something hidden in my subconscious and need to rise.

What is my heart's desire? Is it some kind of a lust that can be seen with the naked eye, or something that I can have for a little while and then I die?

My endeavors were never for material gain, nor did I ask for a life filled with pain, and my search is no longer for fame, for I am Geraldine, "I am" is my name!

CHAPTER 34
"IF I HAD POWERS"

If I had the power that God posses, I can't think of anything I wouldn't put to the test. I would turn the cloudiest sky sunny and blue, and I would make the flowers bloom wherever I wanted them to.

I would restore my youth by turning back the hands of time, and going back to my prime, but it wouldn't take me long to see, that all my powers wouldn't be just for me. I would focus on the earth and the fullness thereof.

Knowing the earth has more money, silver, and gold; than eyes can see or hands can hold. The earth has more than enough to meet the hungry folk's need; and with my powers there wouldn't be a one that the earth didn't feed.

For the rich have treasures laid up in store, but with my powers I would give them to the poor. I wouldn't need honors or a high degree, just the powers to set the innocent free.

Friends would always be true, and come with a heart that's pure. More than that, they would be more than a few and the sick I would make whole and complete.

Embodiments of Truth ~ Geraldine Guy

You would rise above sickness and stand on your feet. For I would use my powers bold and brave, some of the wicked and sinful would even be saved, and many would be kept from the grave.

CHAPTER 35
"A VISION FOR LIFE"

Is life somewhere above the open sky? Because on earth, everyone seems to die! Have we been taught and learned a lie? About the truth of why people really die.

If God gave you a living breathe, whoever said it had to end in death? Do you have faith enough to see? That God is not part of immortality.

We are living in perilous times and are skating on thin ice for not recognizing God, as a God of life. For he is a God of the living and not of the dead,

If you can think logically when using your head. For this is what the Bible has said, "Let the dead bury the dead".

Life is to prosper your soul and the grave was never its goal. The last enemy to be conquered is death, and to "live" will be the only thing left.

CHAPTER 36
"AMAZING IS THE LORD"

Lord, your thoughts are so very deep. You are so gracious with all your ways complete. Full of compassion, you are teaching me your status.

So, I can shine like a rising star, according to thy love. I was made and your mercy has gotten me this far. You told me to delight myself in the abundance of peace, and from darkness of this world, I would cease.

Thank You Lord for being you and keeping me in all I do. You are larger than life, yet your promise is life. How majesty you are to have offered such sacrifice.

You offered your loving son knowing he would be crucified, but you knew His dying would be justified because it was for me He died.

CHAPTER 37
"LOVE TARGET"

Lord teach me how to perfectly love, for perfect love casts out fear, and brings friends far and near! I want love to expand me, this has to be in due time, I plea.

For love will plant me like a tree by the sea and no amount of hatred can consume me. I don't want darkness blocking my view; I want to understand the reality of each and every little clue.

Perfect love will open my eyes, and keep my focus on life higher than the skies. Abundant love is my prayer, more than enough to spare. So people everywhere will know that I care.

Perfect love will put us on one accord, and keep faith strong in the Lord. Oh God, grant this mighty feast, so that all my doubts and fears I will release.

Perfect love that people everywhere will admire and adore, oh Lord, need I ask for more. This is my prayer and it's not amidst. Therefore, quickly Lord and answer I must insist.

CHAPTER 38
"A VIRTUOUS WOMAN"

A virtuous woman is one whom I would call a pleasure to meet. Her character shines deep inside, a woman who barely has anything to hide.

Her morals are as pure as gold and the truth about her, no one really knows, but she is known for her virtuous smile wherever she goes.

A virtuous woman is an independent woman who is strong in her strength and loved by all for the helping hand she has lent.

Her patience is long and her ultimate goal is to do no wrong. She knows how to quench every fiery dot and overcome each and every stumbling block.

This virtuous woman does not come cheap, but one thing for sure, if she is yours, she is for keeps.

She is one with God and knows the truth, which made her free and her only surrender is to victory. I am sure by now that you can see this virtuous woman could be me.

CHAPTER 39
"WHY MUST IT BE"?

Why must it be that no matter what do or humbly say, trouble still seems to come my way? Why must it be oh Lord, that for so long have I cried out to thee, and although I am planted like a tree by the sea. I am still struggling to feel free, why must it be?

Why must it be that the blessing of Abraham are not coming and over taking me? Like you promised in the book of Genesis? I have searched the heaven and the earth. I have looked for you high and low. Now, tell me why must it be that you appear to move too slow? Why must it be that we live in a world where people are so oppressed and full of sin, and nobody seems to be able to bring this corrupt system to an end?

Why must it be that so many feel the need to pretend and put on acts and they can't move forward for the sacks on their backs? They buy fancy cars and all sorts of things they can't afford, and still don't overcome being stressful and bored. Why must it be that so many people are deceived by darkness with their minds running wild, but every time I turn around my own soul is on trial. Am I being chastised? Why must it be?

CHAPTER 40
"I Wonder Why"

For years I have tried to understand this plan God has for man. I wonder why? So much darkness does man penetrates when he was made in God's own image. He was made so great. I wonder why?

And then I wonder why man has conquered everything from right to left, and has not found a way to conquer himself. I wonder why?

I wonder why man so brilliant, brave, and bold. Some so strong and tall, will stop at nothing short or tearing down the Berlin Wall and will lose his soul. Trying to acquire money and gold, the truth about man has never been told. I wonder why?

Man made the ships that sailed the seas and knows how to get honey from the stinging bees. He invented the plane that has wings and flies, and through some mysterious reasons, man still dies. I wonder why?

Man can transplant anything from the liver to the heart, but he still wants to live outside of God. I wonder why? Man has come up with a cure for most diseases, and can do pretty much of what he pleases, but I wonder why? Sickness, man has not overcome and never had a vision of where his healing comes from, I wonder why?

CHAPTER 41
"God Is the Answer"

When through your trials you cannot find peace, God is the answer to your release. There is not a problem too big or small, that God will not answer when you call; yes He is the answer to it all!

When debts are hanging over your head, and you and your family must be fed, just remember what I have said: *"God is the answer"*. No matter what is in the natural we may see, God is the answer and always will be.

CHAPTER 42
"A Righteous Prayer to God"

Lord, I ask that you bless everyone who reads this book and show them a new revelation of your love, power, and mercy. Show them how majesty you are. Father, I humbly pray that there be no rejection of knowledge and no self-doubting. Let them know that wisdom is theirs for the asking and with wisdom comes understanding. Happy is the man that gets, "understanding."

Father, let your people know that you are a rewarder of them that diligently seek you in truth; for you can only be found through the truth of your word.

Father, I truly thank you for welcoming us all to your wonderful throne of mercy and inviting us to call upon you in the day of trouble.

Oh righteous Father, as I bow before you this day, I am standing on your promise to deliver us and your promise to bless the righteous with favor and show us your salvation. Father, I honor you as my every source now Father, I ask for further directions as you increase my knowledge, wisdom, and faith so that I can make a powerful difference in the lives of others.

CHAPTER 43
Questions:

1. *Psalms 104*: "**Bless the Lord, oh my soul. Oh, Lord my God thou are very great.** *How do you bless the Lord?*

2. *What is the first law of God?*

3. *What is an angel?*

4. *What is the promise of God?*

5. Jesus taught in parables. *What is a parable?*

6. *What are the paths of the Lord?*

7. *Isaiah 28:10* talks about precept upon precept. *What is a precept?*

8. *Ephesians 4:24* "**And that you put on the new man, which after God is created in righteousness and true holiness.** *What is holiness? Or what does it mean to be holy?*

God has given us several weapons to use against the enemy's plans for our destruction.

9. *What are at least three (3)?*

10. *What does it mean to be carnally minded and spiritual minded?*

11. *What is good and evil?*

12. *What is the spiritual meaning of Jesus walking on water?*

13. *Who is it that cannot sin?*

14. *What does it mean to be behold?*

15. *What is the biggest concept you can conceive in your head?*

16. *Who are the people that are really happy?*

17. *Where is the one place that you will never find God?*

18. *Worldly people do not understand spiritual laws, so what is the easy way out for them?*

19. *What does it mean to pray?*

20. *Who are the people of God?*

21. *What is the difference between laws and religion?*

CHAPTER 44

"Who They Really Are"

These are true stories about people I know written in poetic truth about their joyous occasions or their Walk through The Valley

1. The Burning Bush President
2. The Day the Towers Fell
3. The Lady Called, "G"
4. A Man Named Leroy
5. Living On The edge
6. Watch Me Make It!
7. So You Think You Are All That!
8. I Know Who You Are
9. The Mannerism of Cassandra
10. She Never Knew How To Move On
11. Blocking Out Reality
12. Strange Man Robert
13. The Mighty Joe Guy
14. A Mighty Wind
15. Making Room for the Groom
16. A Family of Three
17. Yolonda, a miracle worker

CHAPTER 45
"The Burning Bush President"

No offense, but Bush and Cheney doesn't make sense, and I feel sorry for those who stood up in their defense. Bush took over the White House without having to win, and just as he finished picking his disciples, all our troubles began. Bush set in the scorner's seat and took the world into his hands. War on terrorism, he declared was one of the greatest demands. He named his foes for "whom" he wanted revenge. But above all else the war, he wanted to win.

Bush is a President, who came to do or dare, and all over the country, conflict was rising here and there. Bush vowed to get Bin Laden and make him pay, but instead started a Holocaust Day. While killing the innocent and mostly their own. The whereabouts of Bin Laden was still unknown. America was not as blameless as they thought, and Bush didn't care as long as it was others who fought. Bush has no philosophy for life. Because it was never his own, that was offered for sacrifice. Executions and government cuts are his thing. And as long as he is President, FREEDOM will never ring and he will continue to play these cutting games. It is hard for

Bush to understand the needs of the poor, especially, when Enron has been in and out of his door. It is not the President, I detest, but his axles of evil more or less, and the bad seed that runs in his family tree, which runs deeper than most can see. Bush and his disciples are not all degree learned, but the wisdom of God, not a one has asked and earned. So they walk in darkness without light to see them through, and when it comes to leading us, it's not a thing they can do.

For it takes wisdom to lead us into greener pastures, and undo this terrorist disaster. Now listen America and listen well. For it is the truth I seek to tell. America was not attacked without just cause, and the hole they dug was for their own fall. If you examine the facts, you won't have to guess who is responsible for these terrorists' attacks.

It was America and their powerful leaders who assassinated President Kennedy and murdered Dr. King. So please don't tell me their hands are clean. Of course, I hate the war and I don't really know what it is for. I know thirty billion dollars has already been spent, and Bush promised to never relent. I am tired of hearing news about the veterans who dies a war hero, why Bush remains at ground zero. I thank God for freedom of speech. It keeps me from being summoned to the courthouse on 2nd street.

CHAPTER 46
"The Day the Towers Fell"

Loud thundering noises and shrieks upon shrieks
from fearing running voices. The sound of fires,
dreadful sounds, which no man desires. Everywhere
was cries of alarm of the danger that would do so
much harm. It was early day, a little after nine, as
some would say. The towers fell turning lives into a
living hell. There was so much bloodshed and so
many thousands were dead. The World Trade
Center had been attacked, caused by some terrorist
act.

As it came tumbling down, never had there been
such a sight seen on the ground. The Trade Center
had more than a hundred floors, when it collapsed
leaving people trapped on elevators and behind
closed doors.

Oh God, what a terrible sight, it was a day of
darkness without any light. Policeman and firemen
fought with all their might. While risking their lives.
They gave no thought for this day of horror the
terrorists had wrought.

People trembled and cried as wrath and terror fell
by their side. It was a national nightmare, but the
terrorists thought revenge was only fair, as they
planned their revenge and turmoil in the air causing
chaos almost everywhere. Osama Bin Laden, the

Embodiments of Truth ~ Geraldine Guy

President cried, "There is not a cage deep enough for you to hide". So the search was on from zone to zone, but the whereabouts of old Bin Laden may never be known.

CHAPTER 47
"The Lady Called <u>G</u>"

The lady called "G" graces this planet with her calm dignity. Amazon like in her stance, she strides with the pride of the knowingness to converse with her is much like to dance.

In true wisdom, the Lady called "G" is power at it's' fullness. She is powerful, a force to be reckoned with the generosity of her own experience. Only on the surface does she appear indifferent.

Careful words flow from her like verbal music in perfect balance. She creates laughter even when she wants to weep. She is the friend you must keep. Peace in her force. She is lady "G" of course!

Your Friend,

Dee

CHAPTER 48
"A Man Named Leroy"

Leroy is a man who is living a lie, making people think he has a piece of the pie. The rags on his back are really all he owns, and yet so many thinks he has it going on! Leroy works hard at using others to make him appear smart, a good game or so. I think because Leroy didn't have a dime in the bank, for all he makes he spends, only on his habits and life of sins.

Leroy has no fame and people know only his name. He loves putting on acts and keeping people from knowing the facts. Nobody knows he doesn't pay bills, they know he lives in a pretty house that sits on a hill and people know he buys wheels and rims for his shiny new car, and never knew it's a car that never would be paid for.

Leroy is a salesman and good he is, I must say, for he sold a dream to somebody just the other day! Leroy is blinded by the circle he is going in, even ignoring his wake-up call, which may be his last opportunity before his great fall. No doctor in the world could cure his heart of stone. Women love him, but he loves living and being alone. Leroy has a big, round head, and never kept a partner in his bed. For he is like a lion on the loose, looking for his next prey, and he didn't want more than just a roll in the hay!

CHAPTER 49
"Living On the Edge"

Living on the edge is like living on a rough road, where you carry needless burdens and such a heavy load. Living on the edge is like living without spiritual things. You are always in fear what tomorrow may bring pain, because you refuse to use the authority you have in Jesus' name. Living on the edge is like living alone, you have no God, you have no home, and there is no one you can call your own. Maybe you have heard about the Promised Land, and maybe you have felt God's judging hand, and still not know his love for man.

Living on the edge is like living in grieve; you only believe what you can receive. A part of you knows envy and greed, because you have not shared the wealth of your deeds. You operate in a carnal mind, and no matter how hard you try; peace you cannot find. Living on the edge is a way that seems right unto man and the end being death he does not understand. Only on circumstances, does he move and does not care if God approves. Living on the edge, you walk in darkness without faith to see you through; you do not know that everything is possible when God is walking with you. You need His sweet embrace and have refused His Throne of Grace.

CHAPTER 50
"So You Think You Are All That!"

Some people will stop at nothing to gain a position of power, they will even look down on those who clock in and work by the hour. Some will boast and brag and tell you look how the Lord has blessed me; but they are only blinded by the image of what they think they see.

And then there are those who really think they have it going on, have no more than a house, a car, and a cellular phone. People who are not focused usually buy clothes; some will buy more than their closet will hold. For they feel the need to dress to impress and nobody will know their lives is filled with distressed.

Most of their lives are spent plotting up ways to get more money, and when I tell them to put God first they think it's funny! For the love of money, they have such greed of corruption, and they never listen until darkness brings destruction.

They never share the wealth of their deeds, especially if they see you in lack or having a need. They rather give to those who have more than enough. The ones that don't have room for anymore stuff. For no apparent reason they have a way of putting those without in their own spotlight, while thinking to themselves, they must not be doing something right.

They are the ones who walk around thinking they are everybody's good news, but if the truth be told, I would hate to be in their shoes. Yes, they appear to have it all, and they have given no thought that the skeleton in their closet will someday fall.

They choose shadows and worship anyone that carries a title. They don't know that the true and living God should be their only idol, because they have been deceived by the darkness in them and they will go to their graves believing that they really knew Him.

So when you think you are all that and more and you see me as just being poor, brace yourself! I'm the one who heard the knock and opened the door.

CHAPTER 51
"Watch Me Make It"!

I have been at the bottom so doggone long, that some would think that time is almost gone, but now I have to stand on my own.

After going through storm after storm and no matter how hard the wind blew, I kept holding on to the truth I knew. Sometimes too defenseless to fight the battle, yet knowing I had to climb the make-it ladder.

I have had enough of welfare lines and I am tired of scraping nickels and dimes. I dare not press the re-play in my mind; for it makes me realize I have to stop wasting time and claim the abundance that I know is mines.

I have lived a life of chasing bounced checks and making against odd. Now I make just one more prediction, one that will change my life from this self-written fiction. Just watch me make it!

Giving up is not my style and I can't think of anything else that will cause me to throw in the towel. Although, there were times darkness told me I was defeated, but light came and reminded me that it was only that I had been cheated.

People who thought they were all that and more!

Embodiments of Truth ~ Geraldine Guy

Never once helped me open a closed door. They looked down on me with a frown and it was enough to change my whole world around.

My friends stared at me with a question mark in their eyes; not knowing it would be one that I would recognize. Now here I am knowing, I am not what I could be! Nor it am I what I should be, but watch me make and see who I'll be.

CHAPTER 52
"I Know Who You Are"

You are the one that man's mind cannot conceive, because of darkness nor can he believe. Planted in you is God's seed. To save the world is what you need. You are the Son of God. His word has filled your heart. You have no sin, only rivers of waters flowing within. You are conscious of your family being your friend.

Who stick closer than a brother through no end? You are the giver and not the borrower. You are always giving, taking no thought for tomorrow. I know who you are.

You are a gift that can't be bought. You are only giving to others what you have been taught. You are the Shepherd of the Sheep. You are the one that God brings his people to meet. You were sent to set people free. The truth tells me you were sent of thee. I know who you are.

You are the life that God had promised. Nothing can take it, it's in abundance. You walk by faith and not by sight, and never do you walk at night. You are full of wisdom, you are full of knowledge. None of which, came from a college.

You have the power to deal with a man's mentality and teach him true spirituality. I know who you are.

Embodiments of Truth ~ Geraldine Guy

You are wearing a halo around your head. Already you have been resurrected from the dead. God is the word, I am sure you have heard. You are one with God, you are His word. I know who you are.

CHAPTER 53
"The Mannerism of Cassandra"

I write to explain in a language quite simple and so very plain. Cassandra Guy is her name and she has a way of accomplishing the most profound things. Cassandra always has a strong urge to get ahead, I could tell by her logical thinking, when using her head.

Who Cassandra is, I want to make clear for one thing, to me she is quite dear. So, this I want you to hear. I would mention Cassandra loves her share of attention. Cassandra is so well-rounded and so well-spoken, yet, there is not a rule she hasn't broken.

Quite professional she is, and you could always find traces of Martha Stewart where she lives. Cassandra is not your model size, nor is she your big size and most of her beauty is in her eyes. People glanced at what she wore and, heads turned every time she entered through the door.

She would never disclose the nameless designer of her clothes, for she will wear most any that was to be sold. As a matter of fact, Cassandra Guy is some class act; a tough act to follow and the majority of us would never even bother.

CHAPTER 54
"She Never Knew How to Move On"

She was always missing the writing on the wall and kept accepting each and every wasted call. She went to the extreme just to hear whatever was pleasing to her ear.

She gave more than she had to the man in her life and could never face what she knew to be true for it was easier to block out every little clue.

She seem to have forgotten that God is her strength and protection, faced with another ordeal caused by believing lies that could never be real and with her focus gone, she didn't know how to move on.

Her old habits need to be reformed, for she is too smart to appear dumb. If one would search her inner mystery, they too will see; the girl is smarter than you or me.

The things she feels is so obvious revealed. Therefore, I know her dependence on men will one day vanish and her independence will bloom. Lord, help it has to be soon.

CHAPTER 55
"Blocking Out Reality"

What I thought was my oneness, my friend and my protection cause me to block out reality and loose all sense of direction. I thought I was the center of your attention. The skeleton in your closet, the skeleton you failed to mention. You played me like an event, what I called wasted time well spent. How could I have thought you were God sent? But the writing was on the wall, even in your voice every time you called. Still, you fed me line after line that was pleasing to my ear, lines that I gave up all to hear.

You took me up higher than the clouds in the sky; Where I could have stayed except it was up on a lie. Oh' God, why couldn't I have quested? How can I face what I know to be true? Now pain was piercing deep into the depth of my soul: leaving me out of focus and out of control.

The pain was deep and intense; emotions were running wild and love was messing with my mind. A feeling I didn't look for and "God help me", one I never wanted to find.

You walked away without a warning or without any hesitation, now you tell me what you thought was love, was just a long history of dedication.

CHAPTER 56
"The Mighty Joe Guy"

I need you to listen closely while I tell you what I know. This is a short, true story about a man named, "Joe". Joe had a wife and just one child. To really know him, it would take a while. He was never an open book, He was very hard to read and only a few had taken a close look! "Joe" made people believe he was really tough and sometimes thought that was not enough, but what Joe really was, he was successful in his bluff! Joe worked hard and was very smart. He could articulate to the greatest extent and all of his time was very, well spent, and I knew for sure "Joe" was GOD sent!

Although, "Joe" was highly degree learned, most of his knowledge was hard earned. "Joe" would never appear unaware or uninformed, and the more you listened to him, the more you felt dumb. He could hang with the President of the United States if he had to, and if things became too complicated, he would know exactly what to do!

"Joe" served in the Navy as commander-in-chief for many years, now he left us with so many tears! We knew how much "Joe" loved his family and friends, and he loved us to the very end! You, yourself "Joe" were loved immensely and will be incredibly missed, I wish with all my heart, I could give you one last kiss!

CHAPTER 57
"Strange Man Robert"

Come and listen to a story about a man name Robert. Robert is an old and young man who is hard to figure out. He is someone that very, few people really know about. A person of laughter he could never be accused and most of his words condemn and abuse. When it comes to reality of life, Robert is quite dense. However, there are times he can talk and make a lot of sense.

Strange as it is, Robert's mind is filled with negative thoughts and concepts from the past and unknown; and his love for others has yet to be known. He has a certain kind of love for those that's really close to him, but even that sometimes seems to grow dim.

Like the evening sun, his ways are set; something I didn't know when we first met. He appears to be an angel in everybody's sight and everything he does, he will swear it's right.

Robert lives and moves out of fear, making a move only if the threat of death is near. He fears that he will someday hit rock bottom. Therefore, it's hard for him to share as much as a dollar. Still he thinks he is too diverse to read any books, and the power he has is in his looks.

Embodiments of Truth ~ Geraldine Guy

Because his clouded judgment is so airtight, he is being deceived by his own sight and does not understand the principal of living by light. Robert cherishes what he thinks he owns and lives most lonely and alone. I had so wanted to be the apple of his eye, but even that would be a lie, if he is the same old Robert Guy.

It is hard to put a smile on Robert's face and during his upbringing he never learned to embrace. His set-in ways are what I find selfish and sad; but other than that Robert is not all bad. He is like a joke that's not funny and if he was for sale, I would keep my money.

CHAPTER 58
"A Mighty Wind"

A mighty wind blew one day and tried to steal Chiquita's faith away. The strong wind blew hard and disturbed the joy and peace within her heart. Chiquita began to cry with people who really loved her standing close by, for they had called and came from all around to encourage her to hold her ground.

Nonetheless, Chiquita feelings were scrambled and her thoughts scattered, while feeling that her whole world had been shattered, but Chiquita held on knowing that these tests and trials wouldn't stay long.

The weary wind finally gave up and spoke. How can you still be standing Chiquita like bark on an oak? I could hear Chiquita saying, "I know you tried to take my faith away, you blew and blew until you made me sway".

But I have grown stronger since my birth and I am learning how to live faith on this earth. Until now, Chiquita wasn't sure of just how much she could endure. But, now thanks to the wind that blew. Chiquita is stronger than she knew.

CHAPTER 59
"Making Room for the Groom"

Chad and Chiquita if I could define, are two people coming together sharing the same state of mind. For they have captured a very special blessing from above, a blessing that can only be captured if you are in love.

A love that will grow and gives hope for tomorrow, especially when you are sharing both joy and sorrow. Who or what will compare, with the love that Chad and Chiquita will share, and who will even suggest, that they won't be giving and doing their very best.

Chiquita Franklin fashion statement and head strong; took thee Chad Smith and made him her precious stone. She had found her oneness, her friend, and her true soul mate, and apparently she wanted to do a little more than date. So on the 26th of May, they are both looking forward to what's clearly designed as their wedding day, where they have vowed to say "I Do", and a life together they will pursue.

Chad Smith, degree learned and somewhat smart; have made Chiquita, the "darling" of his heart. For she was part of his past, his long coming vision and it didn't take him long to make his decision. So on that special day, will expose themselves for the public view.

Embodiments of Truth ~ Geraldine Guy

Where some, will try to find a flaw, or blemish or two.

As player hater's, friends, and families always do, but they won't have a clue, about what is true, and they can't foresee, that Chad and Chiquita were meant to be!

CHAPTER 60
"Pharaoh and his Family"
"A Family of Three"

There were two (2) Israelites who were in bondage to Pharaoh. They wanted to escape from Pharaoh but didn't know where to go, and because of the hardness of Pharaoh's Heart. The Israelites were forced to pray and seek God.

Pharaoh put heavy burdens on the Israelites and made their work hard, so the Israelites fled from Pharaoh and left him in the dark, but the Israelites knew that Pharaoh accepted enough truth to make him free. So, they came back to where they needed to be.

The Israelites knew the truth of the true and living God, a truth that got rid of the hardness of the Pharaoh's heart.

CHAPTER 61
Answers to Questions (1 through 21)

1. *You Bless the Lord by being what God is. Adore and Thank Him for all his benefits.*
2. *The first Law of God is: to get understanding.*
3. *An angel is someone sent from God.*
4. *The promise of God is "Life". Life has everything you need.*
5. *A parable is something used physically to explain something spiritually. Parables are given to know the mystery of the kingdom of God.*
6. *The paths of the Lord are mercy and truth.*
7. *Precepts are understanding the laws and knowing its' intent. Precepts are from God.*
8. *Holiness is having no evil thoughts. Holiness is not being involved in anything you have to lie about; it is being whole (complete). Holiness is being pure in heart for only the*

pure in heart sees God. A conversation of holiness should never have darkness on it!

9. *At least three weapons to use against the enemy are: God's word, faith, and praise.*

10. *To be carnally minded is death. To be spiritually minded is life and peace.*

11. *Good cannot create evil and evil cannot create good.*

12. *The spiritual meaning of Jesus walking on water means he walked above circumstances.*

13. *Whosoever is born of God does not commit sin, for His seed remaineth in Him, and he cannot sin because He is born of God.*

14. *Behold means to look and listen with understanding.*

15. *"Life" is the largest concept you can conceive in your head.*

16. *The people who are really happy are those whose mind is stayed on thee. Isaiah Chapter 26: verse 3: "and happy is the man that findeth wisdom, the man that getteth understanding".*

17. The place that you will never find God is in the past.

18. The easiest way out for worldly people who do not understand spiritual laws is to reject what they do not understand.

19. Prayer gives God permission to act on our behalf.

20. The people of God are the Living. As God is a God of the Living and not of the Dead.

21. The difference between laws and religion are that they both teach people what they cannot do.

CHAPTER 62
"When It's Love"

To some the definition of love may not be crystal clear, especially if you are in bondage to pain and fear. Real love has no imperfection; it's an affection that the heart feels and it doesn't take a genius to know when it's real.   It can be prescribed as a medication with no side effects; it's the one thing that the body never rejects.

Love is a promise that reassures the soul and can't be bought and can't be sold, still its worth more than any amount of money or gold. Love makes and keeps appointments and does not intentionally leave room for disappointments. Love is everything that the world needs. It's more than just doing good deeds.

Sometimes love is confused with lust, the fantasy of a faithful trust and many find it hard to face when it's gone without a trace. Lust is a strong desire, a hunger, and an appetite within burning like a wild fire. Lust is usually filled with lies and mostly goodbyes. While love is more than a hug or kiss, it's more than any of this. Real love does not change with the passing of a day, and lust is no more than a roll in the hay.

Embodiments of Truth ~ Geraldine Guy

Lust carries, no guarantees, more like a tree that eventually looses its leaves, lust is a thrill needs that's met and fulfilled. While love is too broad to explain, it does not create pain or bring shame and it's more than wearing someone's name, when it's love, it remains the same!

CHAPTER 63
"When Promises Are Broken"

My heart was so settled until you came along. You damaged my emotions, now you have moved on. I remember when we first met one summer afternoon. I even remember how you hummed me all your old love tunes. I was so impressed by your sincere smile, and you promised that we would someday walk down the aisle, if I could, but give you just a little while.

You laid your head upon my breast, and I took you for my shelter nest, while giving and doing my very best. Our love grew and grew and everyday seemed brand new! Oh' my life was so content, for each day with you was a pleasure well spent.

You searched out my inner feelings and taught me that love is giving and forgiving. Now here you were playing those childish games, and it was obvious that things were not the same. You gave every signal that you had changed your mind, but I was too blind to see the warning sign. I tried to block the reality of it out, but you did not leave room for the shadow of a doubt, and not a chance of ever working it out! How could I foresee, what was so invisible to me?

Now, I sit like a junkie in jail, with you holding the keys to my cell. Wondering was it really love or just tormenting hell.

CHAPTER 64
"If I Had Known"

If I had known from the start that it would take so little for us to part. My friends told me there were things I needed to know, but you convinced me it was not so. I had to find out for myself how little there was between us left.

Now, I sit reminiscing the past of a love that I thought would always last. I am remembering your unique style almost as pleasant as your smile. How could I have known it would last for such a short while?

You walked out my door leaving me crying and pacing the floor. I cried like a child. I could even hear my emotions running wild. While the pain echoed in my head, so much emptiness I felt knowing you were no longer in my bed. You told me we were through knowing I had built my whole life around you.

I felt my life had come to an end, and I couldn't bear the thought of starting over again, but now things have changed and my feelings for you are not the same. I passed your house again just the other day. I didn't bother to look your way and if I could turn back the hands of time, never would I entertain the thought of you being mines. If I had known.

CHAPTER 65
Leaving Me without an Invitation"

You left me without a warning, without an invitation. Now you tell me it was not love, but just gratification. You came to me enjoying the warmth within and you decided to leave with only memories of what could have been.

You had settled so deep within my mind, that I never questioned your love for me at anytime. I thought you were the friend I never had, for you always seem to be there when things went from good to bad.

Now I sit listening to the sounds of a drum, not really knowing that it was my heart the beats were coming from. You made me laugh and smile almost like a child. How could I have known it would be for such a short while?

You came to me, you even silenced the storm in my life, and you knew for you I would have made any sacrifice. You were like my yellow and red light, you had my attention, and I would have stopped everything with you in sight.

Still, you left me all the emotional turmoil in my heart, and I do not know how to face our friends and tell them we are apart. What could you have expected to gain, by causing me so much pain?

Embodiments of Truth ~ Geraldine Guy

I thought I was in the songs you seem to hum, or maybe it was just part of the medication of being in your arms. My thoughts of your presence would enhance my soul, something that meant more to me than silver or gold.

Now, you have moved on, with no hesitation of leaving me alone. As to why you left, I had very little information; all I know is that you left without an invitation.

CHAPTER 66
"You Came and Went"

You came to me so righteous and pure, inviting me into your heart knowing you were not sure. You begged me just to meet you halfway, I never had a vision, I would have to beg you to stay. I thought your wanting me was crystal clear.

How could I have known your love was not sincere? You didn't have an excuse for this kind of abuse. You said you'd be the first to apologize and admit you were wrong, but no matter what, you had to move on.

You walked into my life of gladness, and filled my heart with unnecessary sadness. I shared with you my most inner thoughts and gave you my very soul, but got bronze instead of gold. Now, where do I go from here? Knowing that things are never what they appear.

CHAPTER 67
"When Love Hurts"

I wish I knew how this could have happened to me, when all I wanted was to be set free. Free from the yearning of your touch, the hunger of wanting you a little too much.

I don't know how I let you under my skin, after promising and promising myself, it would never happen again. I made such a sacrifice to be the only one in your life, and when my friends warned me. I ignored their advice.

Now, here I sit like a love junkie that can't break free, trying to understand your hold on me; I have been forced to see that there is no more "we"! We have come too far a loose at the seam, and it's more than just some bad dream.

Need my soul be redeemed? Or should I just scream! You were leaving me alone and hurt had made itself a throne, ready to pierce into the depth of my heart and all I can do is cry oh, God!

I don't know what happened to the thrill, could it have been a figment of my imagination, but no it had to be real. Who or what had broken the seal, and how will I survive this distressing ordeal?

CHAPTER 68
"Love Is"

Love is a trial. Love is a test. Love is giving and doing your best. Love is something that you share. It is divided among people who really care. Love is a priceless treasure.

A flowing fountain that can't be measured. Love is like a tree planted by the sea. It is a reflection of you and me. Love is something you can't deny. It shows the obvious, you either laugh or cry.

Love is a memory that never perishes. A thought, feelings to be always cherished. Love is a sound that echoes in the heart. It brings people together and the falseness of it pulls them apart.

Love is an ingredient that's needed in all you do. It's the reality of the real you. Love is unconditional, old, but not traditional. Love is many things; it can bring joy when there has been pain. When there is love, there is always gain.

CHAPTER 69
"Love Builder"

You built our love like some great architect, and then you tore it apart and left me a total wreck. You took me up higher than the clouds in the sky, and brought me down slowly with lie after lie.

Now, I sit pondering my thoughts, wondering what kind of lie I had bought. I look around me and find such disaster, created all because you wanted greener pastures. I could have conquered the world with you by my side; now all that's left to conquer is the emptiness I'm feeling inside.

I believed your promise to never break my heart, and I felt safe letting down my guard. Now, I am paying the price for not thinking twice, you ripped all my emotions away, and left me alone to face each painful day. My pain is so deep and severe, that if you came close, the breaking you could hear.

I now know that heartbreaks have no rules, it will cripple anyone with pain and blues. If only I could turn off the instant replay in my head, I would then erase all that you had said.

CHAPTER 70
"The Power of Prayer"

The power of prayer man must learn to let all his cares become God's concern. For prayer can cause God to move in mysterious ways when we come to him with our humble praise.

Prayer brings every good and perfect gift from above. It puts harmony in your heart and fills you with love. Prayer will turn your situation around and cause you to stand on holy ground.

It will penetrate the darkness around you and cause you to prosper in all that you do. Prayer will lead you out of lack and into plenty, for in my Father's house, the blessings are many.

Man must have a need for prayer, a need to kneel at the throne and meet God there. Prayer brings power and there is no need to pray for hours.

Prayer will save the sick and bring the supernatural answers you need and bring them quick. So when you're facing tests and trials, approach the throne and pray for a while.

Note: *Prayer causes you to expect something from God. Prayer is giving God permission to act on your behalf.

CHAPTER 71
"I Risk My Heart Again"

I feel that I have been caught in a blizzard and I don't know how I am going to make it through. It will take more than I have to get over you!

Like the waves of a tide, you rush to leave my side. Your love for me has become arrogant and inflated with pride.

Bringing my feelings for you to an end; wondering why I had to risk my heart again.

Sadly as it may be, it is over between you and me!

I looked around my lonely room and realized that I had risked another day of gloom.

The stakes were high; the risk was my heart and deep was the lie.

But, if I thought love would let me win, I risk my heart again.

CHAPTER 72
"The Man in My Vision"

Like a diamond in the sky, he caught my glancing eye. I stared all around and stopped because of what I found. I saw his gaze into my searching eyes and knew I had taken him by surprise.

The thought never occurred that I would someday be his bride, but it was the way I stood by his side. His short, black hair streaked with gray, and I had to wonder would he leave or stay?

As I watched him dressed in blue, tall as he was handsome and good-looking too! Now, I wondered what he would do. He had to know available I was for his pursue. Then he spoke in a voice so soft and plain, that I knew my efforts had not been in vain.

And even at that very moment his emotions seem to imply, something even he couldn't deny. I looked at his fingers for some kind of ring, relieved that I didn't see a thing.

I searched the corners of my mind, asking for some sort of sign, the memories was fading that I had left behind and all I wanted was the strength to try one more time, he was the man of my vision. He was one of a kind.

CHAPTER 73
"Love Attack"

I am recovering from a love attack, and I don't need anyone to bring the symptoms back. I'd rather be lonely and blue than risk having another love attack by you! I had no clue what a love attack could do, until I put my trust in you!

Now, you want me to consider letting you come back, never, ever would my heart survive another love attack.

My heart has to mend and the only way it can do that is for me not to let you in. I can't take the chance of it ever happening again. I ignored the rumors but I was hit with the facts, of everything you did behind my back, and it caused the worst of a love attack!

I had bragged to my friends how you were my Casanova, now I dare not face them until my love attack is over! I have to wait until my flashbacks of you are gone, then and only then can I move on!

CHAPTER 74
"A Lifetime Friend"

Who could be a lifetime friend? Who could be loyal with the love and mercy that never ends? Who could share both sad and happy days?

And show their love in many different ways, who could you find on this earth? And how much would a true friend be worth? You could never price a friend too high.

If it was something that money could buy, the gift of a lifetime is a friend for life!

CHAPTER 75
"A Knock on Heaven's Door"

God, I came once more to knock on heavens door, knowing you are my solid rock. Again I knock as I put my hands together and knees hit the floor! I am knocking desperate on heavens door. I just awoke from sleep and slumber praying that my days are not numbered.

My sins are forgiven and laid aside, why I don't feel content and satisfied. I am not understanding why you didn't equal divide? The earth is yours and the fullness you own, but the poverty on earth is mostly known.

I am asking for more than the rest. God, I feel that I deserve your best. Kibbles and bits are not enough. I need more of the better stuff. I need to succeed so I can proceed, to thinking I have done more than any man ever did before, all because I knocked on heaven's door.

Please Lord; I beseech you to fulfill my every need. Nothing to do with greed. A quite moment and all is fair, I take an hour and say a prayer. I pray for others, my health, finances, and more. Is why I keep knocking on heaven's door and experiencing something in my soul forever more?

CHAPTER 76
Yolanda, the Miracle Worker

Yolanda is the mother of three, married to a man who is as good as he can be. Their first child was a baby boy, one that brought them so much joy. The girls came and met their needs, and now they were finished planting their seeds! Yolanda made her life the way she wanted it to be, some she made concealing, and the other parts are quite revealing.

She made more gains than losses, and only worked for a very, few bosses! She made their success and nothing less. I have never known her to make a mess. I see her day view and her characteristics are more than a few. Yes, I do believe I can describe you.

When she walks into a room; the whole room stops and stares! Wondering who in the world just walked in with such a dare! She is a quick thinker with class, perseverance, smarts, and works hard. More than that, she is ambitious, and always held a great position. No knowledge did she lack for all she ever known had come back.

Embodiments of Truth ~ Geraldine Guy

Nobody knows the extent of her treasures, I am sure it's more than one could measure. She does share the good of her deeds and have filled so many needs. Yolanda is my niece, and my dear friend and not one of my foes. I can tell by the smile she wears wherever she goes.

ABOUT THE AUTHOR

Geraldine Guy is the wife to Robert, mother to Robin and grandmother to Victoria. She lives in Memphis, TN, where she's managed to raise her family. Now a retired homemaker she has accomplished so much while being an overcomer of the illness of Sickle Cell.

Geraldine also has learned and understands that she's not a victim of her circumstances. Guy volunteers for several organizations, including Fetal

Embodiments of Truth ~ Geraldine Guy

Alcohol Syndrome and the Sickle Cell Anemia Foundation. She is an advocate for natural pathology and desires greatly to achieve better health and eating habits. Geraldine is very much involved with family and some very close friends in which; the circle of friends share vital information as it relates to health, spirituality, and life in general.

She also enjoys writing letters, spiritual and inspirational themed poems to encourage, inspire, and motivate others along the way. Guy's next journey is penning her next series of poems and stories that will captivate the minds and hearts of those that read the very words that she shares. I am Geraldine Guy. She's a female who has survived many walks through the valley.

www.ingramcontent.com/pod-product-compliance
Lightning Source LLC
Chambersburg PA
CBHW051835040426
42447CB00006B/547